MW01613439

POLAND

ILLUSTRATED BY
KATHERINE OGORZALEK

SIMPLE ETIQUETTE IN
POLAND

By

Krystyna Carter

Simple Books Ltd
Sandgate, Folkestone, Kent, England

SIMPLE ETIQUETTE IN POLAND

Simple Books Ltd
Knoll House, 35 The Crescent,
Sandgate, Folkestone, Kent, England CT20 3EE

First published 1992
© Simple Books Ltd

ISBN 1-873411-30-8

British Library Cataloguing in Publication Data

**A CIP catalogue record for this book
is available from the British Library**

Distributed in the USA & Canada by:
THE TALMAN COMPANY, INC
150 Fifth Avenue
New York, NY 10011

Photoset in Souvenir Light 11 on 12pt
by Visual Typesetting, Harrow, Middlesex
Printed in England by BPCC Wheatons Ltd., Exeter

Contents

POLAND OUTSIDE POLAND

There are an estimated ten million Poles living abroad, and many more if you include the descendants of emigrants from Polish territory. The wave of emigration began in the eighteenth century and turned into a flow in the nineteenth century and also recently after World War Two and in the 1980s. The largest number of Poles are to be found in the USA (around seven million); Chicago has the largest concentration of Poles next to Warsaw. In Canada, the Polish population amounts to 400,000; in Brazil 850,000; Australia 120,000 and in Great Britain around 160,000.

ACKNOWLEDGEMENTS

The author wishes to thank her colleagues at the Polish Cultural Institute in London for keeping her up to date with the good and bad news from Poland. Also her husband, Frank Carter, and his colleagues at the School of Slavonic and East European Studies, University of London, for their comments and suggestions, her uncle, Polo Mróz, in London and many friends in Poland for regularly reminding her of the complexities of Polish etiquette.

Foreword

A sixteenth-century traveller to Poland, William Bruce, noted: '[The Poles]...are large of body, tall, uprighte and personable. The gentry full of ceremonies, civill and courteous in entertainement, bountifull at table, costly in dyett, great gourmandes, and quaffers, not sleepy, nor heavy in their dronkennesse, as the Dutch [Germans], but furious, and guarellsome, high-mynded, and proude...' (Bodleian Library, Oxford, 1598)

I very much hope that if you are able to visit Poland you will be reassured to discover that William Bruce's observations have stood the test of time. You will find, in fact, that all of William Bruce's 'national characteristics' are treated in some detail in *Simple Etiquette in Poland*.

At the same time I hope I have left enough unsaid for the reader/traveller to form an independent view of both the people and country. This is a time of great change when Poland is trying to restore its damaged *past*, catch up with the European *present* and focus upon its *future*. If you are able to manage these three Polish 'tenses' you will know your Poland.

KRYSTYNA CARTER

First Day of Spring, 1992

1

Introducing Poland

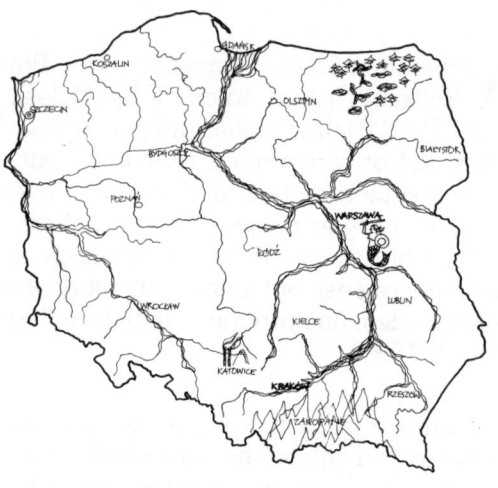

In the words of Juliusz Slowacki, a Polish romantic poet of the nineteenth century, Poland is 'the heart of Europe' - not just geographically speaking, but also as an emotional pulse of the whole Continent.

Poland is indeed located in the heart of Europe. Lines drawn between Europe's extreme continental points will intersect inside Polish territory. It is a lowland country. The average altitude is 173 metres, and only 3 per cent of this area lies above 500 metres. The highest point of 2,499 metres is in the Tatra mountains at Rysy.

There are several thousand lakes and a few mountain ranges. Forests cover just over a quarter of the whole area (27 per cent) and farmland over half of Poland (62 per cent). Most of Poland has a fertile soil, only towards the east and north-east it becomes sandy with marshes and a waste area of glacial lakes.

The climate is moderate, continental with four distinctive seasons. Average annual temperatures range from 5 to 8.5 degrees Celsius, depending on the region. In the summer temperatures can exceed 30 degrees Celsius in the shade, in winter they rarely fall below minus 20 degrees Celsius. Almost all Polish rivers drain into the Baltic sea. The longest are Wisła (the Vistula 1047 km) and Odra (the Oder 854 km). Warsaw is the capital city, other main cities are Cracow, Łódź, Wrocław, Poznań, Gdańsk, Szczecin, Katowice, Bydgoszcz, Lublin.

The country's principal mineral wealth is hard coal, found mainly in the Upper Silesian Coal Basin. Other natural resources are amber from the Baltic, lignite (brown coal), zinc, lead and copper ores, nickel, cobalt, gypsum, sulphur, rock-salt and potassium, and recently new gas finds.

After the amendments to the Constitution introduced on 29 December 1989, Poland's name is not the People's Republic of Poland any more, but the Republic of Poland (*Rzeczpospolita Polska*). It is a democratic legal state. The National Assembly is composed of the Sejm and the Senate elected for a four-year-term. The Sejm has 460 MPs and the Senate 100 Senators.

The President elected by the National Assembly is head of state. The Presidential term of office is six years. The Council of Ministers (government) is the state's supreme executive organ. Its head, the Chairman, is appointed by the Sejm on the President's approval. The Council of Ministers is answerable to the Sejm and the President. Local government is organised through 49 administrative regions and a total number of 50,000 local councillors are elected every four years.

For almost a thousand years the white eagle has been the symbol of Polish statehood. The national emblem is the white eagle with a golden crown set against a red background. The national flag has two colours: white (upper) and red (lower). The Polish national anthem is a mazurka with the first line: 'Poland has not perished yet, we are still here'.

1000 YEARS OF HISTORY

Knowing just a little of the history of Poland will help you to understand many Polish customs and way of life. It will also give you an insight into Polish identification with the cultures of Western Europe.

Mieszko I (960-992) was the first Prince of Poland. He adopted Christianity in 966 and united the Slavonic tribes which inhabited the area roughly corresponding to Poland's present territory into one state. His son Bolesław Chrobry (992-1025) consolidated the new state and became its first crowned king. His successors made up the Piast dynasty which ruled till the fourteenth century, first from the capital of Gniezno and later from Cracow. After the demise of the Piasts the throne went to the Lithuanian dynasty of the Jagiellons. In 1410 King Władysław Jagiełło (1386-1434) fought a fateful battle with the most dangerous enemies of Poland - the Knights of the Teutonic Order - at Grunwald and broke their might.

Poland and Lithuania joined in union and together formed the most powerful dominion of the sixteenth century extending from the Baltic to the Black Sea. The Polish-Lithuanian Commonwealth was to last for more than two centuries, binding together races of different languages and cultures.

The sixteenth century was Poland's 'Golden Age' culturally and politically. Centres like Cracow and Toruń acquired magnificent architecture and developed as centres of art and learning. This was also a century in which the gentry accumulated considerable power and privileges. Such power meant that the Commonwealth was, in effect, a limited democracy, in which no king could ever exercise absolute control.

No middle class emerged in Poland, as happened in the West, so there was no alternative group to challenge the landed nobility and gentry economically or politically. Indeed, their uncompromising independence has left an important mark on Polish behaviour up to this day.

The sixteenth century Reformation came to Poland from Bohemia. Though today a predominantly Catholic country, the Polish Commonwealth had its share of Calvinism, Lutheranism and other Protestant faiths. Poland escaped religious wars and compared to many other European states became a haven of tolerance for many religious denominations. The Confederation of Warsaw of 1573 stated: 'We who differ in matters of religion will keep the peace among ourselves'.

After the death of the last Jagiellon in 1572, Poland became an elective monarchy. The throne went to either Polish aristocrats or members of European royal families. In 1611 King Zygmunt III (1587-1632) transferred the capital from Cracow to Warsaw. The whole of the seventeenth century was a period of wars and anti-feudal rebellions. The Commonwealth began to decline, and the established power of the gentry meant the predominance of a few great families ready to ally themselves with foreign powers.

During the reign of the last Polish king, Stanisław August Poniatowski (1764-1795), many attempts were made to strengthen Poland's economic and political structure. In spite of the fact that in 1772 Russia, Prussia and Austria annexed almost a third of Poland's land in what is called the First Partition of Poland, the king continued to encourage the processes of reform. In 1773 the National Education Commission was set up which was in effect the first ministry of education in Europe.

In 1791 the Constitution of the Third of May was passed by the *Sejm* (Polish Parliament).

This was the most modern and democratic legislation of the eighteenth century, proclaiming complete religious tolerance, giving the burghers the same rights enjoyed by the nobility, recognising Jews as citizens and bringing the peasantry under the protection of the law for the first time.

These provisions, had they ever been applied, would have transformed Poland - if not the whole of eighteenth-century Europe. It was not to be so, for it was inconceivable for the neighbouring powers of Russia, Prussia and later Austria to allow such a democracy to emerge.

Stanisław August
Poniatowski

As a result Russian troops invaded Poland in 1792. King Stanisław August Poniatowski abdicated and the Second Partition of Poland in 1793 between Russia, Prussia and Austria brought more than 120 years of servitude and uncompromising struggle for freedom.

Poland almost ceased to exist on the map of Europe, but never gave up hope. It raised a large army which fought alongside Napoleon, took part in the Spring of Nations in 1848 and twice rebelled against Russian domination in the November 1830 and January 1863 uprisings.

The independent Republic of Poland was reborn in 1918 for a short period of only 20 years. In September 1939 the country was invaded from the west by the Germans and shortly after that from the east by Soviet troops. In spite of this double occupation, Poles developed a very impressive underground resistance movement. A government in exile resided in London and Polish soldiers fought on almost all fronts of the war.

The Yalta agreement signed by the allied powers imposed new frontiers on Poland and the country found itself under Soviet domination and the Communist system. The Polish nation did not accept the new regime. In 1980 various protests culminated in the creation of the independent Solidarity trade union movement. Even the imposition of martial law in 1981 did not stop the process of change and the collapse of the Communist system.

As a result of the Round Table talks in 1989 a non-Communist government was formed. Poland set out on a new road to democracy and reform. The Polish government in exile, after so many years of upholding Poland's rights to independence and freedom, resigned and submitted all the state insignia to Lech Wałęsa in a symbolic ceremony in December 1990.

2

Culture and Customs

Chopin

The traditions of Polish culture are rich and go back to the Middle Ages. The University in Cracow, for example, was founded in 1364 and is one of the five oldest academies in Europe. These days Poland's position on the cultural map of Europe is well established. The Chopin International Piano Competition is organised in Warsaw every five years and attracts talented young pianists from all over the world. Polish contemporary music is also well known with names such as Krzysztof Penderecki, Andrzej Panufnik and Witold Lutosławski. Polish cinema has always been a strong medium with many great achievements coming in the late 50s, especially the work of Andrzej Wajda and Roman Polański and currently with directors such as Krzysztof Kieślowski, Ryszard Bugajski and Krzysztof Zanussi.

Polish posters, miniature graphic art, modern painting and tapestry have won much international praise and Polish experimental theatre has established a strong position on the stages of the world with names like Tadeusz Kantor and Jerzy Grotowski. The contemporary poetry of Tadeusz Różewicz, Zbigniew Herbert and Wisława Szymborska has been translated into many languages including English.

Preserving the traditions of folklore has been of major importance in Poland's cultural policy. Two folk ensembles, Mazowsze and Śląsk, are known for their rich programme of folk songs and dances and their colourful costumes.

Many customs and patterns of behaviour in Poland relate to a Polish sense of honour both real and legendary. A sense of honour for a Pole is not like that of the feuding cultures of Italy, Spain or other Latin countries. It is a matter of grace, high-mindedness, often generosity, defence of the powerless, chivalry towards women, self-esteem and family loyalties. It may also reflect bad features like arrogance, indifference, xenophobia, intolerance and snobbery.

Successive editions of the book by Władysław Boziewicz *A Polish Code of Honour* were available right up to 1939. It contained over 400 principles relating to codes of conduct.

The Polish sense of history is noticeable in the tendency to adhere to the past. A sense of symbolism is also strong in Poland. For a country deprived of freedom for such a long time, communication by symbols became a language in its own right, a custom and a ritual. This is precisely why putting the golden crown back on the Polish Eagle was the most important national event after the fall of Communism.

The Catholic Church, traditional repository of Poland's continuity, culture and national identity thrived in opposition to Marxism. It has played a very significant role in the history and social development of the country. Today, some 90 per cent of the population declare themselves Roman Catholic, but the throes of transition to a market economy, pluralism and commercialism bring new challenges for the Church to deal with.

3

Polish hospitality

'A guest in the house, God in the house' is a sentiment which is widely shared in Poland and reflects the strong Christian basis of everyday life. It is customary for Poles to drop in on each other for a drink or a meal (or both) but always for a chat. Poles love getting together and any excuse will do. An old saying 'Pawn everything, but make a splash' suggests that Poles tend to be the best hosts but the worst savers. Foreign visitors can expect an especially cordial welcome.

As a visitor you should expect to be asked a great many questions about yourself - not because Poles are nosey but simply because they are genuinely interested in you. They may tell you about themselves and their past at length, so be prepared for a number of listening sessions!

Most people in Poland live in flats. Often the flats are small and have to serve many purposes for the family at the same time. The living-room to which you may be invited, for example, might at the same time be a bedroom (often with folded sofas for day sitting) or a dining-room. Poles are very sociable and they will tend to invite you home rather than to a restaurant. Even if you are on a business trip, you can expect an invitation home from your Polish counterpart. [By the way, you will be forgiven if you are late by up to half an hour.]

As hosts the Poles rarely take 'no' for an answer. You will be invited (perhaps entreated) to try this or that dish even after you have said 'no thank you'. To avoid repeated urging to try the dish, you will have to invent a convincing story explaining why it is that you cannot eat it. Otherwise try just a little bit and compliment the cook!

Poles often exchange presents. When they visit each other they invariably bring flowers, books, home-made preserves, cakes and candies, handicrafts, etc. Usually, the presents are inexpensive but thoughtful. Giving a leaving present to a guest is still a popular custom, so do not be surprised if this happens to you.

Children should always be remembered by guests with a small token such as chocolate or a toy. Polish shops still have rather poor facilities for wrapping presents, so if you are bringing gifts from your country be sure to take some nice wrapping paper with you.

When giving flowers do not give chrysanthemums on their own - they are the autumn flowers associated with cemeteries and funerals. However, they can be part of a bouquet. Make sure the flowers are unwrapped when you present them (unless they are in cellophane). Poles are very particular about the number of flowers in a bouquet; they should always be an odd number: 3, 5, 7 etc. Even numbers in a bouquet are only used for the dead at funerals. Decorative flowering plants should be given in a special basket adorned with trimmings. The florist shop will be able to advise you on what to buy when you explain the occasion.

Parties at home are usually around the table. Hard drinks are served undiluted. It is customary to serve vodka throughout the dinner and to keep the bottle on the table. Drinking together is a social occasion and should always be acknowledged by the company. If you raise your glass you look around or turn to your close companion and say 'Na Zdrowie' (pronounced nah zdrovyeh) or whatever toast you wish to make. The rule is, you do not drink as you please, you initiate or you join in. Poles hold forks in a different way and they eat fish with two forks.

If you happen to be invited for a name-day party you will no doubt enjoy the occasion, and may even be invited to share in singing '*Sto lat...*' ('We wish you one hundred years...') an equivalent to 'Happy Birthday'.

Paper cut-outs

4

Meeting People

Poles normally greet each other with the words *dzień dobry* (good day), *dobry wieczór* (good evening) or if they are good friends *cześć* (equivalent to 'cheers') or '*hallo*'. When people ask 'How are you'? they really want to know the answer.

It is customary to shake hands when you meet people and when you take your leave. It is important not to shake hands over the threshold which, according to folk belief, spells bad luck. It is the custom for men to kiss the ladies on the hand on all 'hello' and 'goodbye' occasions. Despite the many changes in today's world, Polish men continue to treat the opposite sex with gallantry: ushering them into a room, helping them with their coats, giving them flowers and frequently complimenting them.

The younger generation is inclined to reject such customs. As a man when shaking hands with a Polish woman you may find that she offers you her hand rather higher than you expect. It is not that she expects you to kiss her hand, it is just an automatic habit. If you however kiss her on the hand, she will be pleasantly surprised, if not impressed, with your knowledge of this custom.

Polish women never really had to embark on what is known in the West as the Women's Liberation Movement. They feel equal to men, and not because Communism brought this idea about. Again history forced the Polish woman to participate on almost equal terms with men in fighting and surviving. Poland is a maternal society and with the worship of the Virgin Mary, the mother figure is highly respected throughout society. In general, etiquette still allows Polish women to enjoy their traditional status and privileges in society, and men seem to like it that way.

If you are introduced to a group of people, you shake hands with everybody. Do not be surprised to see Polish men kissing each other on the cheek, very often three times. This means that they are very good friends or relatives. Poles prefer to express their emotions openly and therefore you will usually have no problem in recognising their mood. It may be helpful to know that the average Pole has a short fuse, is quick to show enthusiasm and is quite spontaneous!

The Poles do have a good sense of humour, especially political. However, they are not that keen on slapstick-type humour and you will not see much of it anywhere in Poland.

Keeping your hands in your pockets when talking is seen as rather rude by Polish standards, unless the person you are speaking to knows that in certain countries it is a sign of feeling relaxed.

Birthdays in Poland are usually very private family occasions and not celebrated as much as they are in other countries. You will not be expected to send birthday greetings to a Pole and it would even be difficult to find a special 'birthday card'. The Polish custom is to celebrate the day of the saint after whom the person is named. If you look at the Polish calendar you will see that every day of the year is devoted to at least two names, for example 29 June is for Piotr and Paweł, 12 August is for Klara and Lech, 4 November is for Karol and Olgierd etc. The name-day is a big social occasion both at home and at work. Everybody remembers it with greetings and small gifts.

5

Food and Drink

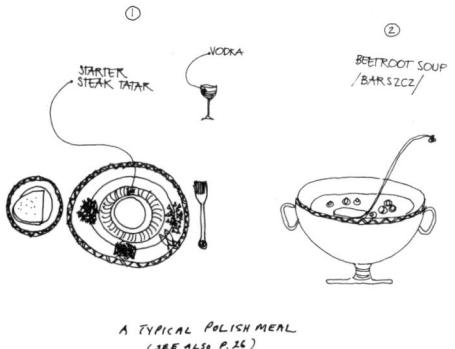

STARTER STEAK TATAR

VODKA

BEETROOT SOUP /BARSZCZ/

① ②

A TYPICAL POLISH MEAL
(SEE ALSO P. 26)

You may find Polish cuisine rather heavy. Lots of lard and butter are used for frying and the food can be rather starchy. (Take your indigestion tablets to be on the safe side). Since World War Two Polish cuisine has deteriorated, mainly because of the nationalisation of most of the catering trade. Eating out, therefore, was not much fun in Communist Poland. Fortunately, the art of cooking traditional Polish specialities has been preserved in many homes and there is no doubt that the standard of cuisine will improve in the coming years. Following the privatisation of the catering trade, there is already a noticeable improvement in the quality of food served in restaurants and bars.

Your hotel breakfast will almost certainly be of the continental type, but you will have a choice. It is worth sampling some of the delicious Polish sausages or the many home-made soups and stews:

Barszcz (Borscht) - a beetroot soup usually served with a kind of ravioli,

Bigos - a sour cabbage stew with many kinds of meat,

Pierogi - savoury or sweet dumplings filled with meat, cheese, fruits or forest mushrooms.

Polish cakes and gateaux are a splendid combination of domestic, French and Austro-Hungarian traditions and are worth trying.

Look for small private restaurants and cafeterias or try the following most recommended high-class restaurants:

Bazyliszek - in Warsaw, Old Town Market Square (old Polish cuisine)

Wierzynek - at Cracow's Main Market Square 15 (traditional - high-class)

Pod Łososiem - in Gdańsk, ul Szeroka 54 (sea food)

Adria - Poznań, ul. Głogowska 14 (regional)

Ratuszowa - Wrocław, Market Square 7 (traditional).

You may be served your tea without milk in a glass. Milk in Poland is usually boiled, so trying to make 'traditional English tea' with it is not to be recommended! Coffee may also be served in a glass; it is not dissimilar to Turkish coffee with a sediment at the bottom.

Watch how much you drink in Poland and try not to mix the 'grain and grape'. Poles drink vodka in a 'bottom up' fashion; it is important, therefore, to eat while drinking.

Mariacki church, Kraków

6

Business Matters

The recent political changes in Poland have led to rapid moves towards a market economy. The Polish government has embarked on a wide-ranging programme of privatising and restructuring state industry. The most successful so far is 'privatisation by liquidation'. The only choice for the country is between going full speed ahead and sinking where it is. The reforms suggest that Poland is moving forward. In addition, her geographical position between Western Europe and the Soviet Union with 500 kilometres of coastline on the Baltic (and from there access to Scandinavia and the North Sea) can be seen as being very well placed for European trade.

In 1990, tens of thousands of new businesses were registered, including about 5,000 foreign businesses. Foreign investors may operate in Poland in any branch of the economy either as a limited liability company or as a joint stock company. Banking facilities for such businesses are constantly being improved and a shake-up is also taking place in foreign trade financing, where more and more banks have now been granted foreign exchange licences and a new Export Development Bank has been set up.

Poland is keen to encourage foreign investment. But you would always be well advised to check the current legislation on conducting business in Poland, as the law is evolving alongside all the other restructuring processes taking place. If you are involved in business in Poland you should certainly study the Foreign Investment Law reformed in 1991 to the benefit of foreign investors. Obtaining reliable Polish legal advice as well as professional translating and interpreting services is also likely to be important in any business context.

Securing a contract in Poland may take a long time. The Poles are still suspicious of being taken for a ride, and they are very cautious about taking risks. A knowledge of the Polish language (however basic), an understanding of their culture and mentality and a full-time presence in Poland by members of a negotiating team will ensure that your efforts are not wasted. The main difficulty in finalising a contract is likely to be concerned with how the deal is to be financed and paid for.

Time has never meant money in Poland. For a Polish person time is an abstract philosophical concept. You may still find that letters are left unanswered, decisions delayed, opportunities missed, appointments postponed at the eleventh hour, people responsible are absent or difficult to find. Poles are still best at improvising and not at all bad when forced to meet deadlines.

Telecommunications in Poland are still very backward, and the whole system is undergoing general modernisation. At present less than eight out of 100 inhabitants have a private telephone and around 8,000 Polish villages are without one. You can easily telephone from the hotel and usually there will be telex and fax services available there; but if you are on the streets the situation is more difficult. Remember you require tokens for use in public telephone booths which you can buy at kiosks.

Because of these telecommunication problems, it is advisable to give your Polish hosts as much information in advance about your business plans as possible: send a telex, tell them what and whom you wish to see. If you leave the whole organisation of your visit to them you may not get what you want.

After years of a centrally-run economy, Poles are only now learning how to adopt new managerial skills, including decision-making and undertaking personal responsibility. You may find yourself facing either a perfect Western-style management team or one that is still following the old ways - talking to too many people leading to no concrete results. Do not imagine that the Iron Curtain has been, or is being, replaced with a mirror reflecting the West.

Western businessmen who are only looking for a quick profit in Poland are better advised to stay at home. Western currency is too precious for the Poles to allow out of the country easily. Companies that are willing to accept a mixed package of payment, hard currency plus Polish Złoty, stand a much better chance of being successful in Poland. Polish currency can be used within the borders of Poland for further investment (at the recently opened Stock Exchange) or to purchase goods for export.

Going to Poland on business unprepared is a waste of time. You would be well advised to take advantage of getting to know as much as you can in your field before you go. Talking to Polish expatriots living in your country or seeking information from academic sources known to you, approaching official Polish tourist authorities or diplomatic and commercial missions can all contribute to your 'data base' and also help build your self-confidence.

Hotels in Poland are scarce and the prices for accommodation are therefore very high. If you plan to travel to Poland frequently you might be better off renting a flat. With business privatisation in Poland this will not be difficult. Polish newspapers usually carry advertisements some of which are in English; there are also many recently-formed accommodation agencies ready to help. There are a number of papers published in English which can be purchased in hotels or kiosks which are found everywhere. Some of the more interesting publications are: *The Warsaw Voice, Gazeta International, The Insider, Polish Business Voice, Contemporary Poland, Project, Theatre in Poland, Art and Business, Polish Music.*

Cloth Market

The Złoty is Poland's currency unit. The smallest unit is the Grosz (1 Zł = 100 Gr.). Polish money consists of 13 banknotes of roughly the same size (similar to the US dollar) ranging from 50 to 1,000,000 Złoty as well as a large range of coins. Foreign currency is best exchanged in the banks or Bureaux de Change (in Polish *kantor*). The current exchange rates are always displayed and it may differ from *kantor* to *kantor* or from region to region. The Złoty is convertible and can be changed into foreign currency. There are certain Customs restrictions on the money you take out of the country. The general rule is that you cannot take out more than you brought in, but you should always check on arrival with the Customs Officer. (March 1992: $1.00 = 13,000-14,000 Zł.).

Postage stamps are sold at post offices (*poczta*) and at some kiosks. Post offices are open 8 am to 8 pm except Saturdays and Sundays. In large cities one post office is usually open 24 hours a day.

7

Work Days and Holidays

The working day begins quite early in Poland, factories start at 6 am, and offices between 7.30 and 8 am. There is no official lunch break, and the working day finishes after 8 hours at 2, 3 or 4 pm. This is when you can expect rush-hours on public transport and on the roads. It is also the time for a working woman to do her shopping on the way home. Grocery shops usually open quite early at 6 or 7 am and stay open till 7 pm. Department stores are open from 9 am till 7 pm, bookshops from 11 am-7 pm. There are more and more small private shops emerging and some of them operate 24 hours a day (in big towns only).

Under the old regime, when Saturday was a free day it really was free, with almost all the shops being closed too. Now they are open on Saturday, usually until 4 pm.

Schools close for the summer holiday at the end of June and reopen on 1 September. Schools in Poland have two weeks holiday for Christmas, one week for Easter and two weeks in February between semesters. Students of higher education start their academic year in October, they have Christmas and Easter breaks and a longer winter break in January. They finish in June.

Compulsory schooling starts at the age of six. Elementary schooling takes eight years, secondary education can be for three years (Vocational school) four years (Lyceum) or five years (Technical). *Matura* is the matriculation examination taken on the completion of secondary education (except at Vocational school). To enter higher education candidates have to go through quite a difficult entrance examination.

1 January - New Year's Day
Easter - Sunday and Monday
1 May - Workers' Day
3 May - National Day (to celebrate the 1791 Constitution)
Corpus Christi - always Thursday either at the end of May or early June
15 August - The Assumption of Our Lady
1 November - All Saints Day
11 November - Day of National Independence
25-26 December - Christmas.

Travel

Old Warsaw

There are frequent flights to Poland by the main international carriers. The Polish Airline is LOT. The main airport is Warsaw - Okeçie. By Western standards it is very basic indeed. Checking in your luggage does not mean that you will part with your suitcase. It will be waiting for you on the other side of the counter, so do not go straight into the waiting lounge, find your case and go with it through the security check.

On arrival you will go through passport control (prepare yourself for a long wait during high season), then collect your luggage from the conveyor belt and go through either green (nothing to declare) or red, if you have goods to declare. Even if you have no goods to declare you will be asked to fill in a form stating the amount of money you are bringing into the country.

But take heart: Warsaw's new international airport is due for completion in 1992 and it is expected to meet international standards. With Poland's central position in Europe, Okęcie II airport will be able to help relieve the growing congestion of Western European airports. This vision of the future is central to the LOT privatisation plans.

Poland can also be reached, of course, by train, coach or sea depending on where you live. Information about travelling to Poland is available from any of the Polish Tourist Office ORBIS Information Centres around the world, as well as from travel agents. Poland is keen to put herself on the tourist map and the ORBIS network is in the process of being privatised.

Poland is a country of many natural spas. They are usually situated in picturesque areas and it is customary for Poles to take advantage of these health resorts as often as possible as either in- or out-patients. The most popular spas are Krynica, Ciechocinek, Kołobrzeg, Busko, Wieliczka, Iwonicz, Świeradów, Polanica. Polish spas cater for a multitude of ailments including respiratory, circulatory, locomotive, rheumatic, coronary and gynaecological conditions. Treatment is available for foreign visitors. ORBIS offices will be able to give you detailed information.

British citizens who take their National Health Medical Card can obtain reciprocal free emergency treatment in Poland. Citizens of other countries should seek advice at their embassies or consulates. A pharmacy in Polish is called *apteka*. No foreign prescriptions are accepted there, but you can buy some analgesics, influenza medicines, gastric drugs etc. over the counter.

DOCUMENTS

You will almost certainly need to arrange a visa to visit Poland. The formalities usually take on average two weeks. You should have a passport valid for at least nine months from the date of application and remember to have at least one clear page on which your visa may be stamped. A fee has to be paid for the visa. It is advisable to apply for a multi-entry visa if you plan to travel frequently to Poland.

CUSTOMS REGULATIONS

Poland is not in the EEC, although the country signed the EEC Associate Membership in 1991. Visitors can bring to Poland the following duty-free items: personal belongings, gifts not exceeding the value of $200 (1991 regulations), alcohol – 1 litre of wine and 1 litre of spirits (except pure grain), 250 cigarettes or 50 cigars or 0.25 kg tobacco. Other articles should be declared. Narcotics and weapons are prohibited. When going out of the country, visitors can take the following duty-free: gifts with a total market value up to $200 (1991 regulations), up to 250 cigarettes or 0.25 kg tobacco, 5 litres of alcoholic beverages, and works of art provided that they date from after 1945 and are accompanied by a letter from the appropriate authorities (though this law is now being discussed and a relaxation of the regulations is expected).

CREDIT CARDS AND TRAVELLER'S CHEQUES

The following cards are accepted by nearly 500 establishments in Poland: American Express, Diners Club, Eurocard, Mastercard, Access, JCB, Visa and Air Plus Cards. In many instances you can use them for paying your hotel accommodation and in high-class restaurants. ORBIS branches will accept these cards for tourists services, tickets, car hire etc.

DRIVING IN POLAND

The roads are reasonably good (though motorways are scarce), as is the network of petrol stations, but lead-free petrol is still only

available in the larger towns. Colour codes for fuel are as follows: red - 98 octane, yellow - 94 octane, green - 86 octane. The letters 'ON' stand for diesel. Traffic regulations are similar to those in most countries of Europe. Remember that in Poland you drive on the right. The following speed limits apply throughout the country:
- motorways 110 km/hr.
- other roads up to 90 km/hr.
- densely-populated areas up to 60 km/hr.
- with a caravan trailer up to 70 km/hr.

To drive in Poland you must be in possession of your car registration documents, an international driving licence and the Green Card.

The classification of roads in Poland is: E - for international highways, followed by the

Toruń

number of the highway (E20); T - for national highways, followed by the number (T15). Surfaces are adequate on main routes; secondary roads tend to be narrow and badly lit.

Give way to the right where no road has priority. At roundabouts priority is from the right. Trams have priority crossing roundabouts.

The blood-alcohol limit is strictly enforced at zero. Police are entitled to take you for a blood test as well as demand on-the-spot fines for speeding and similar offences.

There are no restrictions on travelling within Poland. Many cities are linked by a comprehensive public transport network (plane, train and intercity coaches). Polish Railways - PKP - offer a good and reliable service and is relatively cheap. All large towns have buses, trams and trains. Tickets for your municipal transport should be bought in advance at the kiosks. There is no conductor service, you cancel your ticket in the automat on the train or bus.

Taxis are marked with an international Taxi sign. Some are commissioned by hotels to take care of guests and will display the name of the hotel. Charges are metered and the amount of Złotys is multiplied by the officially fixed rate. This rate is displayed in the taxi. It is almost impossible to hail a taxi on the street. Instead find the nearest taxi stop.

Electricity

220 v, 50 cycles. Sockets are the continental type with 2-pin round, so you should take adaptors with you.

Tips

Approximately 10% of the bill in restaurants, hotels, barber shops, cafeterias, taxis etc.

USEFUL ADDRESSES AND TELEPHONE NUMBERS

Ambulance - 999
Police - 997
Fire Brigade - 998
These calls are free from any telephone, but they are unlikely to be answered by English-speaking operators.

Car breakdown service - 987, 954
Ordering a taxi - 919
Operator (international calls) - 901
Operator (domestic calls) - 900
Visas (extensions) - 603 68 78 or 603 68 46

Ministry of Culture and Art - 20 02 31
Ministry of Foreign Affairs - 28 74 51
Ministry of Foreign Economic Relations - 693 50 00
Ministry of Finance - 20 03 11
Ministry of Industry and Trade - 21 03 51
Ministry of Environmental Protection - 25 00 01
Ministry of National Education - 29 72 41
Main Statistical Office - 25 32 41

Polish Academy of Sciences - 20 02 11
Conference of the Polish Episcopate - 38 92 51
Polish Student Association - 26 93 26
Polish Red Cross - 28 43 38
Polish PEN Club - 26 39 48

Wawel Castle, Kraków

USEFUL ADDRESSES

British Embassy, Aleja Róż 1, 00-556 Warsaw.
Tel: 28 10 01.
The USA Embassy, Aleja Ujazdowskie 29/31,
00-540 Warsaw. Tel: 28 30 41.
Canadian Embassy, ul. Matejki 1/5, 00-481
Warsaw. Tel: 29 80 51.
Australian Embassy, ul. Estońska 3/5, 03-903
Warsaw. Tel: 17 50 81.
Belgian Embassy, ul. Senatorska 34, 00-095
Warsaw. Tel: 27 02 33.

ORBIS INFORMATION CENTRES

POLORBIS Travel Ltd.,
82 Mortimer Street,
London W1N 7DE.
Tel: 071 636 2217 or 071 637 4971, Fax: 071
436 6558

ORBIS - Polish Travel Bureau Inc.,
500 Fifth Avenue,
New York, NY 10036.
Tel: 39 10 844, Tlx: 14 83334

ORBIS agent in Canada - Kentours,
296 Queen Street West,
Toronto 28,
M5V 2A1 Ont.

Polish LOT agent in Australia,
Suite 1801, 388 George Street,
Sydney.
Tel: 232 8430

Polish Embassy in Great Britain,
47 Portland Place,
London W1.
Tel: 071 580 4324

Polish Embassy in Australia,
9 Turrana Street,
Yarralumba ACT,
2600 Canberra.
Tel: 73 12 08

Polish Embassy in Canada,
443 Daly Street,
Ottawa, Ontario.
Tel: 236 04 68

Polish Embassy in the USA,
2640 16th Street,
N.W. Washington.
Tel: (202) 234 3800

Polish Cultural Institute,
34 Portland Place,
London WIN 4HQ.
Tel: 071 636 6032

UNITED LINGUISTS,
Translators and Interpreters,
8 Quantock Gardens,
London NW2 1PH.
Tel: 081 458 6434 or 081 449 8049
Fax: 081 458 3227 or 081 447 1854

9

Useful Words and Phrases

SIMPLE POLISH DICTIONARY

yes	*tak*	(tahk)
no	*nie*	(ñeh)
please	*proszę*	(prosheh)
excuse me	*przepraszam*	(psheprahshahm)
thank you	*dziękuję*	(dzhehnkooyeh)
good morning/ afternoon	*dzień dobry*	(dzhehñ dobri)
good evening	*dobry wieczór*	(dobri vyehchoor)
good night	*dobra noc*	(dobrahnots)
see you later	*do zobaczenia*	(do zobahchehnah)
Mrs	*Pani*	(Pahñee)
Mr	*Pan*	(Pahn)
left	*lewo*	(lehvoh)
right	*prawo*	(pravoh)
post office	*poczta*	(pochtah)
Solidarity	*Solidarność*	(Solidharnosytsch)

ACCOMMODATION AND FOOD

tea	*herbata*	(hehrbahtah)
room	*pokój*	(pokooy)
breakfast	*śniadanie*	(syñahdahñeh)
bed	*łóżko*	(wooshko)
bathroom	*łazienka*	(wahzyehnkah)
cafeteria	*kawiarnia*	(kahvyahrñah)
restaurant	*restauracja*	(rehsthawrahsts-yah)
bill	*rachunek*	(rahoonehk)
bon appetit	*smacznego*	(smahchnehgo)
free	*wolny*	(vohlni)
occupied	*zajęty*	(zayehti)

TRAVEL

taxi	*taksówka*	(tahksoofka)
car	*samochód*	(samohoot)
driving licence	*prawo jazdy*	(prahvo yahzdi)
surname	*nazwisko*	(nahzveesko)
train	*pociąg*	(potshonk)
plane	*samolot*	(sahmolot)
arrival	*przylot*	(pshiloth)
departure	*odlot*	(odloth)
railway station	*stacja kolejowa*	(stahtsyah kolehyovah)
platform	*peron*	(pehron)
ticket office	*kasa biletowa*	(Kahsah Beelethova)

10

Did You Know..?

Spa Nalorzow

The population of Poland (*Polska*) amounts to 38 million inhabitants (23 million in 1945) and it places the country in 7th position in Europe and 25th in the world. The density is 120 people per square kilometre, two-thirds of them living in 830 towns and cities. Graduates make up 8 per cent of the total workforce. Poland has a relatively young population - nearly one-third of her inhabitants have not yet reached working age. The average life span is 67.2 years for men and 75.3 for women. There are 105 women for every 100 men. There are about 12 divorces per 100 marriages.

Poland is a country in which the population contains over 96 per cent Poles. Ethnic minorities, mainly Ukrainians and Byelorussians account for 450,000, Germans 500,000 and Jews 10,000 (1990 data).

The language belongs to the Slavonic family of languages like Russian, Bulgarian, Serbo-Croat, Czech and Slovak. Polish, unlike some other Slavonic languages, does not use the Cyrilic alphabet, it uses Latin letters.

GREAT POLES YOU SHOULD KNOW ABOUT

1. Nicolas Copernicus (1473-1543) - the discovery of the heliocentric shape of the universe: *De revolutionibus orbium coelestium*.
2. Tadeusz Kościuszko (1746-1817) - Polish and American General. Fought in the American War of Independence. In 1794 made Commander of the armed forces of the national insurrection in Poland.
3. Frederick Chopin (1810-1849) - composer: two concertos, 58 mazurkas, 17 polonaises, 21 nocturnes, 26 preludes, 27 etudes and other forms.
4. Maria Skłodowska-Curie (1867-1934) - winner of two Nobel Prizes: co-discoverer of polonium and radium.
5. Józef Konrad-Korzeniowski - Joseph Conrad (1857-1924) - an outstanding English writer born in Poland.
6. Karol Wojtyła - Pope John Paul II - first non-Italian Pope in 455 years, formerly Metropolitan Archbishop of Cracow.

Others include: Adam Mickiewicz (1798-1855) a romantic poet, professor at the College de France; Kazimierz Pułaski (1747-1779) the Polish and American national hero; Ignacy Paderewski (1860-1941) a famous Polish pianist and one of Poland's Prime Ministers in the inter-war period; Czesław Miłosz (born 1911) contemporary writer - a Nobel Prize winner in 1980 in literature, and of course Lech Wałęsa.